A NEW MINDSET FOR FORGIVENESS

Getting Rid of Grudges, Resentments, Unforgiveness, Bitterness and Blame

GREG AITKENS

A New Mindset for Forgiveness
Copyright © 2023 by Greg Aitkens

All rights reserved. No part of this publication may be reproduced, distributed, or transmitted in any form or by any means, including photocopying, recording, or other electronic or mechanical methods, without the prior written permission of the author, except in the case of brief quotations embodied in critical reviews and certain other non-commercial uses permitted by copyright law.

Tellwell Talent
www.tellwell.ca

ISBN
978-0-2288-9449-0 (Hardcover)
978-0-2288-9448-3 (Paperback)
978-0-2288-9450-6 (eBook)

TABLE OF CONTENTS

Introduction v

Chapter 1: What Is Forgiveness, Anyway? 1
Chapter 2: What Happened to Cause Hurt and Pain? 4
Chapter 3: Why Did the Offenders Do What They Did? 13
Chapter 4: How Do We Feel about What Happened? 17
Chapter 5: What about All That ANGER? 23
Chapter 6: Actions and Acting Out..29
Chapter 7: Coming to Our Senses...32
Chapter 8: What Prevents Us from Wanting to Forgive? 35
Chapter 9: What Does Jesus Want to Teach Us?..........................39
Chapter 10: Studying the Scriptures...43
Chapter 11: Deliverance from the Bondage of Evil Spirits.............49
Chapter 12: Tools and Resources for Forgiving Others 55

More Resources on Forgiveness...77
About the Author..79

INTRODUCTION

"And I will give you a new heart, and I will put a new spirit in you. I will take out your stony stubborn heart and give you a tender, responsive heart."
—*Ezekiel 36:26*

Years ago, I was cheated and betrayed badly by a man I trusted. I thought this man might be the father figure I'd been looking for—the father I never really had. Nothing could have been further from the truth.

Being cheated and betrayed was very hurtful, and I was devastated by the events that transpired. I was shocked by this man's lack of sensitivity or concern toward me. I was shocked by his inability to admit to any wrongdoing. The others who were part of the betrayal also refused to admit any responsibility for what occurred. This only added to the betrayal and created a lot of anger and pain in me.

I found myself yelling at God in my frustration. "How could you allow this to happen to me? What did I do to deserve this treatment? What are you going to do with these cheaters so that no one else gets hurt? When are they going to be held accountable?"

I felt trapped and anxious. I was at my wit's end and had no clue what to do. For a while, it was difficult for me to even function normally. I was damaged goods. I was in great pain.

I thought about taking legal action. I was ready to continue to confront those who were involved and demand an apology. I wanted to receive restitution for the substantial amounts of money owed to me. Instead, the Lord orchestrated a change in my workplace that allowed me to flourish and learn many new things. Eventually I was able to channel all the rage I felt into new and positive goals that served others. Even after all these years, I'm still benefitting from what was set in motion decades ago—after I "shook the dust off my feet" from the people who had injured me so badly.

Twenty years after this betrayal, I gave a talk to a Christian group in Palm Desert, California. One of the themes in the talk was based on Ezekiel 36:25-27. The key was verse 26:

> "And I will give you a new heart, and I will put a new spirit in you. I will take out your stony stubborn heart and give you a tender, responsive heart."

You could hear a pin drop as I shared from my heart about the ongoing struggles in forgiving I still carried with me after almost two decades.

As we broke into small discussion groups, I noticed that just about everyone had a story like the one I had shared. Many participants admitted to harboring some level of unforgiveness with certain people in their lives. Up until then, I kind of assumed that I was the only person who struggled mightily with unforgiveness.

This was an important realization for me, and it motivated me to begin to put together some ideas for others who struggle with unforgiveness.

In 2017, my wife Ginny and I moved to Cambria, California, a small, quiet town near the ocean. It was a big change from our very busy, if not frenzied, life in Orange County, California, where we had lived for almost forty years.

Once we had relocated, I had a "nudge in the back" from God to write a book on forgiveness. I hadn't done much writing like this before—and certainly nothing approaching a book. I was a financial advisor in Orange County, not a writer or author.

However, as I continued to feel that nudge from God, I began to write a book on forgiveness. My early attempts were mostly venting and complaining about others with whom I'd had problems. Over time, the book became a "workbook" suitable for doing live workshops. Over the last few years, I've been conducting live workshops, with between twenty and for forty people in each one. The participants were all members of Christians in Commerce (now Worklight.org) and their guests.

Our Lord worked powerfully in these four-hour workshops. I continued to refine and update the workbook so others could benefit from the process of forgiveness Our Lord took me through over many years.

Next, our daughter Irene facilitated the creation of my website called www.EntertheHealingRoom.com. It has videos, reflections, and several tools designed to assist anyone struggling with forgiveness issues.

The book you are about to read is for anyone who'd like to learn more about forgiveness. There are specific questions at the end of each chapter to help the reader be better equipped to handle forgiveness issues that will pop up in life. We all run into challenging and difficult people who say and do hurtful things, and we need to know how to forgive them.

CHAPTER 1

What Is Forgiveness, Anyway?

From my perspective, there is a lot of confusion about what forgiveness is, and what it is not. So, let's start by defining forgiveness. Forgiving—whether others or ourselves—is one of the most important tasks we could ever accomplish in our lives. Let's take a look:

Forgiveness Is NOT:

- overlooking, ignoring, or denying what happened to me
- excusing or condoning the damaging behaviors of others
- trivializing the trauma or pain I experienced
- forgetting the hurt and harm I sustained, or pretending it did not happen
- restoring trust with an offender or feeling that I need to have an ongoing relationship with that person

I like British philosopher Joanna North's definition for forgiveness:

> When unjustly hurt by another person, we forgive when we overcome the resentment we carry toward the offender, not by denying our right to resentment, but instead by trying to offer the wrongdoer compassion, benevolence, and love. As we freely give these, we as

forgivers realize the offender does not necessarily have a right to these gifts.[1]

What Does True Forgiveness Look Like?

True forgiveness means that we let go of:

- Anxiety and anguish over failed or broken relationships
- Judgments, condemnations, or bad-mouthing our offenders
- Hatred, or wishing others were dead
- The desire for revenge, retaliation, or the need to "settle-the-score"
- Being distracted by hurtful events of the past
- Replaying our grievance story with anyone within earshot (or ourselves)
- Constant anger and seething rage
- Being obsessed with grudges, resentments, bitterness and blame

When we exercise true forgiveness, we let go of statements like:

- "What they did was unforgivable!"
- "Forgive____? Not on my watch! I will NEVER forgive them!"
- "I will get___, if it's the last thing I ever do."
- "I don't get mad—I get even!"

Instead, we can develop a mindset of forgiveness:

- "The past is gone. What's done is done. It's now ancient history".
- "The past events were unfortunate, but they are a part of life."
- "Life is too short for harboring any ill-will toward anyone."
- "I'm moving on with life."
- "I'm letting this go."
- "I'm being set free."
- "God will settle the score. He will judge, so I don't have to."

---

[1] Robert D. Enright, PhD, *Forgiveness Is a Choice: A Step-by-Step Process for Resolving Anger and Restoring Hope* (Washington, DC: APA LifeTools, 2001), 25.

These words from 2 Samuel 22:17–20 provide encouragement:

> He reached down from heaven and rescued me; he drew me out of deep waters. He rescued me from my powerful enemies, from those who hated me and were too strong for me. They attacked me at a moment I was in distress, but the Lord supported me. He led me to a place of safety; he rescued me because he delights in me.

For Reflection

1. Define *forgiveness* in your own words.
2. What has happened in your life that requires you to exercise forgiveness?

CHAPTER 2

What Happened to Cause Hurt and Pain?

A huge part of moving on from the hurts and pains we sustain in life is being able to look soberly and honestly at what happened. This is the first step in uncovering what may have been buried in our subconscious for years.

My Forgiveness Story

My own forgiveness story began in childhood.

I grew up in what is classically described as a dysfunctional, alcoholic family. Both of my parents were very heavy drinkers. I remember a lot of fighting and arguing, most of which was initiated by my mom. She was critical of everybody and everything. She had come from an alcoholic family in Scotland, and her father was a mean drunk.

As the oldest child, I felt like I received the brunt of my mom's criticism. This caused many fights between us. I have described the environment as a kind of World War III on a daily basis between Mamma and me.

My dad was a hard worker, but he barely made enough to support the family. The basics of life were there, but there were no extras. Early on, I took on paper routes and gardening jobs to earn some much-needed cash.

For many years after I grew up, I felt that my dad had abdicated his role as my father, leaving his oldest son (me) to deal with his wife (my mom). There was much yelling and many doors slammed in anger, and no one ever apologized. The environment was neither nurturing nor encouraging.

I somehow sensed that this family environment was NOT how family life was supposed to be. From the time I was about twelve years old, I was gone from home a lot—at school, at the ball field or basketball courts, or at other friends' homes. I knew something was just not right with my homelife. I didn't want to be there, and I only went home to eat, sleep, or study. It was traumatic to be there because I knew there would be another argument with my mom.

Years later, after becoming a Christian, I realized that Jesus had reached in and saved me in two ways: First, He made sure I was GONE from home a lot so I wouldn't absorb the regular criticism my mom would direct at me, and I wouldn't have to witness my parents' regular drinking bouts. Second, he provided me with the strength to "stand my ground" with my mother. Even as a young boy, I learned to fight back and NOT take in all the criticism she loved to dish out. My motto at the time was "I'm just not going to put up with this from her." It was an important coping mechanism for getting through all the ugliness.

Miraculously, I managed to survive childhood; however, the damage had been done, and I buried it all deep within me. I was very angry with my dad for allowing all this to happen. And I was angry with my mother for never encouraging or supporting me in anything I did. There were NO "hugs" happening at our house.

My two younger siblings stuck around to absorb all the dysfunction. They did not make themselves absent as much as I did. They both suffered tremendously from this chaotic environment.

My brother Keith who was two years younger, died about two years ago. Unfortunately, he was diagnosed with juvenile onset diabetes and spent his life dealing with this nasty disease. My mother "doted on him," never really teaching him how to properly care for his own physical issues. In addition to all the psychological challenges of living in our family, the years of improperly taking care of his disease came back to haunt him—in fact, this killed him.

My sister is eighteen years younger than I am. I was pretty much gone from home when she was born, so we never really formed much of a relationship. She has led a very difficult life and is now in her mid-fifties. My theory is that many of her problems are rooted in unforgiveness, directed at our parents. In my opinion, she has adopted a victim mindset, which affects everything she does. I pray that she can move past her unforgiveness and be set free.

My unresolved anger at my parents caused me to get angry very quickly over minor life events or become defensive and snarky with my wife. All of this came from the "unfinished business" I still carried regarding my parents. My loving wife deserved NONE of this treatment from anyone, especially from her husband. Clearly, something needed to be done. I needed to change.

The Encounter with Christ and Healing of Memories

In November 1985, I learned that my dad had died suddenly at work of a heart attack. I wasn't quite sure how to react because I had been so angry with him for many years (I was now in my thirties). A few months after he died, I attended a weekend retreat sponsored by a wonderful ministry called Christians in Commerce. While on this retreat, I discovered how angry I was with my father and really came to terms with it. That weekend, a very mature man—who would become a good friend and mentor—asked me to pray with him for my dad and my mom. He led me in a prayer of forgiveness. Through several miraculous events on this retreat, I was introduced in a very personal way to Jesus Christ. That encounter really changed my life for the better, and I began a new friendship with our Lord and Savior.

A few years later, though, I realized that I could still become very angry, very quickly. I sensed there was more work to be done in forgiving my dad—but I had no clue how to go about it. My friend from the retreat suggested that I go to Tempe, Arizona, to visit a friend of his who had a ministry called the Healing of Memories. I trusted my friend, so I decided to make the trip, still not really knowing what would happen.

Byron was my trained counselor and guide for the Healing of Memories. The first day was tough; I was asked to remember many of the unsavory and hurtful aspects of growing up. All of the many not-so-great experiences during childhood were right in front of me again, after being deeply buried for many years. However, my attitude was that whatever it took to move on and forgive was OK with me.

Fortunately, I was able to connect with a good friend in the evening for good Mexican food and a few beers, which helped to provide solace from dealing with all the difficulties of remembering a traumatic childhood.

Byron had encouraged me to attend a morning Mass at Our Lady of Mount Carmel in Tempe, Arizona. By then, it was clear to me that the purpose of my time with Byron was to forgive my dad, even though it was unclear to me how that would happen.

The church in those days had a huge crucifix that hung from a skylight structure in the ceiling. As I prayed about my next steps, I noted that the crucifix had a lot of amber colors in it. What was I going to do? How could I forgive my dad? What could I do to allow forgiveness to happen?

Suddenly, I heard a voice within me that said: "You are going to need to cry." Surprisingly, this message was completely OK with me. I responded to Jesus by saying, "Whatever it takes to forgive—I'm OK with that. *You* are calling the shots."

Soon after, I met again with Byron. We were talking about ways to forgive my dad. I was still bound up and stuck, not making any progress. Byron suddenly said: "Greg, there is nothing else I can do for you. You will just need to pray."

Byron left, and I found a corner of the room where I could kneel and pray. I was feeling anxious and confused, and I couldn't focus on much of anything for fifteen or twenty minutes. I later realized that this time was probably an attack from the evil one, who does not want us to forgive anyone.

Suddenly, I saw a clear vision that surprised me. I saw my parents and me in a three-way hug; we were completely enveloped by a soft, amber-colored plastic wrap. Remember the color of the crucifix at the church? Yes! That same amber color!

This vision was surprising because I don't ever recall a hug like this while growing up. I vividly remember fights, rancor, and many arguments, but no hugging or affection of any kind.

Shortly after seeing this vision, Byron returned, and I shared what had just happened with him. I think he was surprised as well. He then said: "Greg, I think you are ready to forgive your dad."

We talked a bit more, and within a short time, I was crying like a baby. These were tears of release and new freedom. All the years of pent-up anger and frustration and disappointment were now all gone.

Ever since I experienced this healing of memories, I've noticed that I can't become angry with my dad, even if I try. I could no longer find ways to criticize him. I learned that my dad had grown up with a mean drunk father himself, which meant that he carried a lot of pain from his own childhood. He did the best he could under the circumstances.

What about Mom?

But what about my mom? Wasn't she the one I really needed to forgive based on all the problems I had with her? It's a fair question!

Rightly or wrongly, I felt that my main issues revolved around my dad—due to his absence as a father figure. I figured (wrongly) that all the wonderful works of Jesus regarding my dad would just kind of "apply" to my mom as well. I operated with this belief for many years; however, I finally realized that I needed to go back and address the unforgiveness I was still carrying toward my mom.

I knew more work had to be done because often when my wife would say something to me, I would react in a defensive manner. I could swear that it was my mother saying my wife's words to me! This was totally unfair to my great wife, and I knew I needed to "clear the decks" regarding my mom.

A few years ago, I had a quiet, prayerful conversation with my deceased mother. She had died about eight months after my dad passed away, in 1986. I basically told her that she no longer had any influence on me whatsoever, and I told her that I forgave her for all the harsh words and criticism she had hurled at me for many years. I told her that I knew she, too, had come from an alcoholic family, which explained a lot about her own critical words and behaviors. As the saying goes, "Hurt people hurt people." Her lashing out at me was a direct indication of all the unresolved pain she still lived with from her own childhood. This helped me to cut her some slack and finally move on and forgive her.

Here is the bottom line from my childhood:

- I witnessed lots of excessive drinking and drunk adults.
- I was heavily criticized by my mom. This was painful.
- There was a lot of fighting and arguing and rancor—and no apologies ever.
- My dad abdicated his role and left me to deal with mom. To me, this was very unfair.
- Our home environment was hurtful and caused me pain and damage.
- I became convinced early in life that this kind of family life was NOT normal. I suffered from guilt and shame about my own family.

- By the grace of God, I survived my childhood and became a fairly normal human.
- Years after my parents' deaths, I worked hard to forgive both of them. Today, I'm really glad I did.

Another Episode of Hurt

I went to work in the financial services business in the early 1980s. I was part of a major West Coast life insurance firm in Newport Beach, California.

Subsequently, I worked with a small firm where people I trusted cheated and betrayed me. What happened was unfortunate and unfair. These episodes were upsetting and made me angry, and they created a lot of hurt and pain in me.

Through a lot of quiet contemplation and prayer, I was eventually able to move on. In fact, in a very profound way, Jesus told me to leave where I was and find a new firm, with new people to work with.

About that time, I met a man named Don. We quickly became good friends. He introduced me to a new firm, which I learned quickly was a far more honorable place to work. Working there was like dying and going to heaven after experiencing the hurt and devastation of the previous firm.

To summarize this episode:

- I was cheated and betrayed, and it was unfair.
- I did not insist on getting agreements in writing. I was very naïve.
- I was very angry and bitter for many years over this entire experience. I harbored GRUBB (Grudges, Resentments, Unforgiveness, Bitterness, Blame) about this episode for way too long.

- I was to blame as well for not checking out my colleagues more thoroughly.
- I learned what not to do and who not to be through this traumatic experience. Learning these lessons became very helpful to me later in life.

When we face into the hurt and pain we're carrying, we can review what happened to us, and the following words may apply.

We could have been:

- Cheated
- Abused
- Unjustly treated
- Taken advantage of
- Harshly criticized
- Betrayed
- Abandoned
- Ignored or overlooked
- Subjected to vile and obnoxious behaviors

Other people could have been:

- Cranky, snarky, or rude
- Control freaks and manipulators
- Selfish or even narcissistic
- Arrogant, haughty, and full of themselves
- Bombastic bags-of-wind who love to hear themselves talk
- Mean, nasty, or vicious
- Petulant and insisting on getting their way
- Bullies on a giant ego trip
- Boorish and overbearing
- Completely inflexible
- Insensitive to others
- Angry and filled with seething rage
- Vindictive and vowing to exact revenge

- Obsessed with their own self-image and overly concerned about "how they look"
- Always right? They just know it all!

For Reflection

1. How were you unfairly treated?
2. What things cause you to be hurt or wounded?
3. Who is the one person you have had the most difficulty forgiving?

CHAPTER 3

Why Did the Offenders Do What They Did?

As I began to process the hurts sustained in my own life, I thought about the possible reasons others were so offensive and hurtful. I truly wanted to understand the motivations others had for what they did or said. This kind of understanding has helped me a lot to moving more toward mercy, compassion, and forgiveness. Here are a few insights I've gleaned:

They embody the maxim "Hurt people hurt people." Most of us have met people who have been profoundly wounded by the words and behavior of others. Many remain in great pain, even after many years. If they have not come to any resolutions or closure regarding their own pain, they will often lash out at others and say and do things that are hurtful to others. All the venom they harbor inside has to come out, and we may be the unfortunate and undeserving recipients of their rage, harsh words, and nasty behaviors.

In my experience, many folks who have been profoundly hurt haven't found ways to move on, or let the past go. Many are miserable, angry, sad, lonely, or depressed. They are truly STUCK in unforgiveness, and they may not even know it.

Some years ago, I met a lady who was part of the same service club I belonged to in our community. I quickly discovered that she could be quite nasty, even vicious in her words and actions—even in the middle of meetings. She had strong opinions about everything, and she liked to get her own way. I learned that she had suffered from a lot of traumas in her life. It appeared to me that these events remained very unresolved in her own mind. I suspected this was the reason for her lashing out with such offensive words and behaviors.

Have you met some hurt people in your own life? Are you a hurt person yourself, still harboring events from the past?

They didn't know what they were doing. Some people seem to live in their own altered reality. They are insensitive to others and oblivious to their own words and actions. They are so focused on themselves that they are completely unaware of the effect they have on others around them.

A former manager I worked for was all about making money for himself. He seemed to feel entitled to it and didn't seem to care about the very people who were lining his pockets with hard-earned revenue. He also could be very vindictive. If others did things he didn't like, he immediately went on a "warpath" to get even. I don't think he really knew what he was doing.

Luke 23:34 says: "Father, forgive them, for they don't know what they are doing." These are the very words Jesus used when he was being nailed to the Cross at Calvary. Our issues with others cannot begin to compare with what Jesus had to endure.

They have a tainted outlook or are caught up in the ways of the world. One of the founders of Christians in Commerce had a relevant reminder: "That Christianity is one thing, but this is business." In so many cases in my own professional life, I've seen many people, including Christians, "check their Christian values at the door" when entering their place of business. They say and do things to enslave themselves to the "almighty buck"; they are obsessed with making more money and becoming successful in the eyes of the world. This relentless worldly ambition can often cause them to say and do hurtful things to others. They are oblivious to anyone but themselves.

Over many years as a financial advisor, I regularly attended seminars on various topics to ensure I was staying current with laws, regulations, and opportunities I could discuss with my clients. In too many cases to count, the "sales" presentations made to us were filled with inaccurate information, frequently boasting about investment returns that were just not true— or not disclosing enough about the true risks of a potential investment. I became far more discerning in the process of finding good programs for my clients. I wanted to act as my clients' intermediary in finding sound investments.

They are ignorant of God and Christian values. I'd been in the market for a specific kind of car. I saw one available at a dealership, but it was about 150 miles away. I decided to make the trip anyway. I scheduled an appointment with the salesperson to check out the car.

I arrived at the dealership to learn that the car I was interested in had been sold the night before! I received no communication from the salesperson so I could have avoided making the long drive. I think he figured I could be easily swayed into buying a different car, which was not true at all.

Making that long drive was disappointing. If he'd contacted me the night before, I could have avoided more than six hours of driving.

After talking to the manager, they agreed to fill my car with gas. The salesperson apologized.

Now it's my job to forgive him.

They shift the blame to others. Some people excuse their bad behavior as follows: "I come from long lines of raging alcoholism (or some other family dysfunction); these were the cards I was dealt, and there is nothing I can do to change it." We all know this is patently false and points to this person's unwillingness to make changes in their behaviors.

Sally came from an alcoholic family. She went through a painful divorce in her early twenties. She was angry about her life and bitter and resentful about what had happened to her. She continued to make horrendous life decisions on many fronts, and today she is a ward of the government living in Section 8 housing and receiving food stamps. She is convinced that her issues are the fault of her parents (both of whom were alcoholics) and that she could never elevate her own standing in life. She frequently lashes out at others and demands money or attention. She plays the victim really well. She blames her situation on her family of origin.

They blame their behavior on wiring, nature, and proclivities. A false rationale for bad behaviors from offenders might be: "Well, this is just the way I am, and I cannot (or will not) make any changes in myself for the better. What you see is what you get with me, so you just better get used to it!"

Like you, I've been around some people who love to control everything and everybody around them. They are largely oblivious to the way their own words and actions impact others. Their wiring and nature compel them to always want to be in control.

For Reflection

1. Why do you think the people who harmed you did so?
2. What do you need to understand about those who injured you?

CHAPTER 4

How Do We Feel about What Happened?

In my own journey of forgiveness, I eventually decided it was important to revisit exactly how I felt about the things that caused me hurt and harm. Many people want to ignore this important step. We might:

- Deny what really happened.
- Pretend it didn't happen, and just "shove it to the side"
- Bury (swallow) the wounds deep inside ourselves
- Continue to harbor seething rage, which is eating us alive
- Attempt to ignore all the raw emotions which are raging within us
- Determine we will "deal with this later" and delay taking action

The predominant feeling I had upon reflecting on harm from others was anger. It all just made me really mad. In a lot of cases, the words and actions of others were unnecessary and totally unjustified. Others acted badly or said awful and hurtful things, and anger in me at those offenders is what flowed first.

About eighteen months ago, I attended a board meeting for a local service club. Big decisions were being made that night concerning a huge upcoming event. One other board member got very belligerent and nasty, and some of his frustration (and a childish tirade) was directed right at me. I was tempted to react in anger, and to this day, I'm glad I didn't. Twenty-four hours after the incident, I did send an email to the other board member, highlighting his contentious behavior and relaying that his words and actions were NOT appropriate in any way. Fortunately, our friendship was restored over time. It was not any fun to experience what happened.

Anger is a dangerous emotion with many tentacles that are just not good for us. I'm devoting the entire fifth chapter of this book to the topic of anger. It's important for us to know how to deal with our anger.

Other feelings I've witnessed and felt personally are hopelessness, despair, and dismay over what happened. In so many cases, the hurtful words and behaviors of others just come out of left field. We were not expecting nasty and vicious words directed at us. We might retreat to a mental location deep within ourselves wondering, *How could this happen? Why did it happen? What did I do to deserve this?*

Tony, a friend of mine, had a rocky relationship with his mother. She made his childhood very chaotic. He was never quite sure what to do with "Mom." As I got to know Tony better, I noticed that he would *disappear* for days or weeks at a time. He would not respond to calls or emails. He finally admitted to me one day that he was taking medication for depression and was experiencing side effects. His depression was due to a lot of unresolved baggage and unforgiveness regarding his mom. He had buried all his anxiety deep within and felt powerless to move on in life. What could he do? He needed to work on forgiving his mom.

An encouraging Scripture is in 2 Corinthians 4:8–9:

> We are pressed on every side by troubles, but we are not crushed. We are perplexed, but not driven to despair. We are hunted down, but never abandoned by God. We get knocked down, but we are not destroyed. Through suffering, our bodies continue to share in the death of Jesus so that the life of Jesus also is seen in our bodies.

The bottom line is that when we think we are at the end of our rope, we are never at the end of our hope. God does not abandon us.

Here are more great reminders from Psalm 34:15–18:

> The eyes of the LORD watch over those who do right; his ears are open to their cries for help. But the Lord turns his face against those who do evil; he will erase their memory from the earth. The LORD helps his people when they call to him for help. He rescues them from all their troubles. The LORD is close to the brokenhearted; he rescues those whose spirits are crushed.

During these times of despair, Our Lord is ready and available to us. He is the source of power, courage, and wisdom, and he helps us get through all our problems. We need to LEAN on Our Lord. Will we invite our Lord Jesus to help us?

Another common feeling after hurt and harm is a desire for revenge. We might want to:

- Get even and settle the score
- Retaliate in kind, inflicting the same or worse pain on our offenders
- Tell "them" what they did and how we really feel about it—getting out the *Bazooka Blaster*
- Insist on an apology before anything else can happen

A great example of revenge is portrayed in the somewhat dark Irish movie *Banshees of Inisherin*, which tells the story of two former friends who are now out to get each other. They become enemies before our very eyes. We see fingers cut off, a house burned down, animals killed, and several relationships ruined as a result of grudges held and the mutual desire for retaliation. During the movie, we never really see them mend their ways, apologize, or seek forgiveness. We see all the ugliness of revenge in living color.

Another feeling we can have from hurt and harm done to us is victimization, cloaked around the short question: "Why me?" Here some common feelings from the "I'm a victim" mindset:

- Why did this hurt and harm happen to me?
- What did I do to deserve this kind of treatment?
- Where were you, God, when all this bad stuff was happening to me?
- How dare that offender treat me in this manner!
- Don't you want to feel sorry for me?

We can all be guilty of plotting revenge. During the many years when I was nursing the hurt and harm done to me, I was NOT thinking of ways to reconcile or resolve issues or "turn the other cheek." For way too long, I told myself, "I will get even—if it's the last thing I ever do!" I sure had the desire to "tell the other person off" and inflict as much harm and hurt back on the offender as possible. I wanted them to feel every bit of the pain I had sustained.

Plotting revenge, of course, is the opposite of what Our Lord desires. He wants us to move on without resorting to physical violence or continued harsh judgments. He provides us with the tools we need to move past revenge.

The Scriptures help us once again with good reminders about NOT seeking revenge:

> For God called you to do good, even if it means suffering, just as Christ suffered for you. He is your example, and you must follow his steps. He never sinned, nor deceived anyone. He did not retaliate when he was insulted, not threaten revenge when he suffered. He left his case in the hands of God, who always judges fairly. (1 Peter 2:21–23)

> Dear friends, never take revenge. Leave that to the righteous anger of God. For the Scriptures say, "I will take revenge; I will pay them back," says the Lord. (Romans 12:19)

Another set of feelings from harm we have sustained are anxiety, aggravations, and regular agitation. Why do we harbor these feelings? Reasons may include:

- The incidents around our harm remained unresolved and unreconciled.
- We sense that there is unfinished business. We don't have closure on certain relationships involving harm that was done to us. Our wounds have not healed.
- We have not received apologies we feel we are owed, nor have the offenders admitted to any wrongdoing.
- Attempts at confronting our offenders have ended badly. Nothing has gotten resolved. These attempts may have made things worse, like stirring a hornet's nest.

These feelings can cause the following (they certainly have in me!):

- Being easily annoyed over minor events in life
- Having regularly dour and negative attitudes about many aspects of life
- Going ballistic over minor life events
- Being short, rude, caustic, or nasty with others
- Exhibiting defensiveness regarding any input we receive and perceiving these as attacks
- Whining, moaning and complaining about what is going on
- Using angry, foul language, which can be an indicator that things are just not right "under the hood" (*inside* of us)
- Living JOYLESSLY and scoffing at the small things which can make us happy
- Expressing ongoing and persistent negativity, criticism, and judgments of others

Robert is a fellow I know who is frequently in a bad mood. He shared that a fellow he didn't like married his mother after his father passed away. Robert exhibits little joy, and he is often cantankerous and unfriendly. I want to ask him, "What the heck happened to you to cause you to be so irritable all the time?" I suspect that some of his outlook is due to unforgiveness.

Let's review how we feel. We mentioned five predominant feelings we might experience after we sustain hurt and harm. We all feel differently. The ones we examined are:

- Anger and rage
- Hopelessness and despair
- Desire for revenge
- Victim mindset, feeling sorry for oneself
- Anxiety, aggravations, and regular agitation

For Reflection

1. How do you feel about the hurt and harm you have sustained?
2. In what way or ways are you still living with one or more of the five feelings above?

CHAPTER 5

What about All That ANGER?

We humans can get very angry when we are hurt. When we are cheated, betrayed, abused, or abandoned unfairly, it can make us mad. While harboring this anger, we can be easily annoyed, aggravated, bothered, or displeased. We can go ballistic over minor life events.

While in state of anger, we might exhibit the following:

- We are off-balance, not our normal self.
- We feel devastated by the words and behaviors of others.
- Our well-being has been destroyed; we are way off-kilter.
- We easily can explode into a fit of rage.
- We are anxious and not sure what to do.
- We are distracted by past hurtful events.
- We might be plotting revenge—to settle the score on our terms.
- We might be angry at ourselves for "allowing" the hurt to occur.
- We feel imprisoned by all the rage within us.
- Our physical and mental health suffers.

I've seen two reactions to intense anger from profound hurts:

1. *External*: An angry person lashes out at others. Remember, "hurt people hurt people." Venting and ranting out loud is common. They have a lot of complaints and will blast anyone who disagrees with them. They can be negative and critical about many aspects of their lives. Many people are just rude,

caustic, short, or cantankerous. They can be downright nasty, vicious, or mean.

I used to work with a person who was very angry all the time. He'd frequently complain bitterly about things going on in his life. His rants were loud and filled with profanities. He didn't seem to experience much joy in his life. My colleagues and I had to wonder: What the heck is going on with this guy? What unresolved issues could cause these levels of anger on a regular basis?

2. *Internal*: An angry person just "swallows" their rage and buries it deep inside. They might be sad, lonely, in despair, or depressed.

What they do not realize is that they are destroying themselves from within. They live with seething rage, and while they can put on a public "game face" to attempt to hide the inferno inside, their manner and tone with others tells a very different story.

> Of the seven deadly sins, anger is possibly the most fun. To lick your wounds, to smack your lips over grievances long past, to roll over your tongue the prospect of bitter confrontations to come, to savor the last toothsome morsel both the pain you are given and the pain you are giving back—in many ways it is a feast for a king. The chief drawback is what you are wolfing down is yourself. The skeleton at the feast is you.
>
> —Frederick Buechner[2]

Another aspect is the anger we may still have toward ourselves. Some common self-talk might be:

- "Boy, how stupid I was to get taken advantage of . . ."
- "What was I thinking?"

---

[2] Frederick Buechner, *Wishful Thinking: A Seeker's ABC* (San Francisco: HarperOne, 1993), 117.

- "What possessed me to join up with ___?"
- "Why the heck would I do that?"

We need to come to terms with our own anger. Confessing my own wrongdoing before God and others has helped me a lot, and so has asking for forgiveness from God and others. But then we have to accept the gift of this forgiveness for ourselves. This really helps to set us free.

We could also be directing our rage at God. We might blame God for our issues. We could be asking:

- "Lord, how could you allow this to happen to me?"
- "Where were You when all this was happening?"
- "What are You going to do about this situation?"
- "Lord, are you going to allow this person to get away with what they did?"

In reality, God is not to blame for the hurtful words and behaviors of other people. It is the sin and wrongdoing of others committed against us that is the problem. God is weeping along with us at the harm-causing antics of others.

What Do We DO about All This Anger?

I'll end this chapter with eight practical ways to deal with our anger so we can move past it and live a life free from its negative effects.

1. **Realize the damage we are doing to ourselves.** It's been said that when we are resentful and holding a grudge, it's like drinking poison, but hoping the other person dies. Unrelenting anger *is* poison, and it can destroy us physically, mentally, emotionally, and spiritually. The Apostle Paul offers great advice in Ephesians 4:31–32:

    > Get rid of all bitterness, rage, anger, harsh words, and slander, as well as all types of evil behavior. Instead,

be kind to each other, tenderhearted, forgiving one another, just as God through Christ has forgiven you.

2. **Seek the help of Jesus.** A great Scripture is found in Matthew 11:28-30. Jesus said:

> "Come to me, all of you who are weary and carry heavy burdens [like anger!], and I will give you rest. Take my yoke upon you. Let me teach you, because I am humble and gentle at heart, and you will find rest for your souls. For my yoke is easy to bear, and the burden I give you is light."

While we may be stuck in unrelenting and seething rage over past events, Our Lord is inviting us into a closer relationship with Him. He wants to help us; all we need to do is ask.

3. **Write a "Vent Letter."** Writing notes about what happened is very therapeutic. It allows us to transfer all the rage we're feeling on to the paper in front of us. It's for our eyes only, not to be shared with anyone else.[3]

> Understand this, my dear brothers and sisters: You must be quick to listen, slow to speak, and slow to get angry. Human anger does not produce the righteousness God desires. So get rid of all filth and evil in your lives [like anger!], and humbly accept the word God has planted in your hearts, for it has the power to save your souls. (James 1:19–21)

4. **Seek God's forgiveness for all the ways we may have contributed to the problems in prior failed relationships.** Did we let our pride get in the way? Did we fan the flame of discord, rancor, animosity, or hostility by our own words and actions? We need to confess our

---

[3] I developed a process called the *Vent Letter Plus*. You can find it at EntertheHealingRoom.com, on pages 36–38 of the Workbook you'll find there.

own sins. We then can receive forgiveness from God. Psalm 51:1–3 can put us on the right track:

> Have mercy on me, O God, because of your unfailing love. Because of your great compassion, blot out the stain of my sins. Wash me clean from my guilt. Purify me from my sin. For I recognize my rebellion; it haunts me day and night.

5. **Discern whether or not we are angry at ourselves.** Are we still steeped in guilt and shame over our own words and actions from the past? We need to move on from our anger and let it go. The past is the past, and we all make mistakes. Let's seek God's help in forgiving ourselves and be willing to accept His forgiveness.

6. **Capture every rebellious or angry thought.** In 2 Corinthians 10:5, Paul encourages us this way: "We capture every rebellious thought and teach them to obey Christ." Whenever we are tempted to go down the path of anger, we quickly remember to capture our thoughts, and we remind ourselves about who we are becoming in Christ. Psalm 19:14 also provides great instruction: "May the words of my mouth and the meditation of my heart be pleasing to you, O Lord, my rock and my redeemer." We cannot experience the favor of God while we harbor anger.

7. **Understand the Offenders.** It's really hard to understand why people do what they do, especially when other people's anger and bad behaviors are unfairly directed at us. In recent years, I've tried harder to understand why others said what they said or did what they did. In many cases, this has helped me to have empathy for what others have endured in life. I've even thought that if I'd been in their shoes, I might react in a similar fashion, or even worse. This has helped me to feel mercy and compassion, cut others some slack, and remember how much mercy the Lord has poured out on me. As James 2:13 says, "There will be no mercy for those who have not

shown mercy to others. But if you have been merciful, God will be merciful when he judges you."

8. **Get rid of the devil!** The evil one loves to tempt us to cling to our anger and never forgive anyone. He likes nothing more than to see us remain in bondage to the dangerous emotion of anger, which is rooted in unforgiveness. Chapter 11 covers the topic of deliverance from evil spirits. Here are a few Scriptures which can assist us with expelling the tactics of the evil one:

- So humble yourselves before God. Resist the devil, and he will flee from you. (James 4:7)
- Don't let evil conquer you, but conquer evil by doing good. (Romans 12:21)
- Give all your worries and cares to God, for he cares about you. (1 Peter 5:7)
- We use God's mighty weapons, not worldly weapons, to knock down the strongholds of human reasoning and to destroy false arguments. (2 Corinthians 10:4)
- A final word: Be strong in the Lord and his mighty power. Put on all of God's armor so that you will be able to stand firm against all the strategies of the devil. (Ephesians 6:10–11)

For Reflection

1. Think about something that has happened in your life that still causes you to feel angry and hurt. What steps have you taken to release all that anger?
2. Of the eight practical tips in this chapter, which one do you feel inspired to implement over the next few weeks? Write in your journal any benefits you receive.

CHAPTER 6

Actions and Acting Out

When we have been wounded by others, the hurt and harm we've experienced can cause us to behave in less-than-ideal ways. We're often unaware of just how much the hurt and harm we've endured in the past affects our present attitudes and actions. In this chapter, we identify some of the ways we try to numb our unresolved pain. Taking an honest look at ourselves opens the door to God's grace and mercy to work in our souls.

1. **Abusing alcohol or drugs.** I watched my own parents drink excessive amounts of alcohol on a regular basis. I frankly wonder to this day how we arrived back at home safely after the gatherings we attended as kids, as many of the adults were "three sheets to the wind."

Since both of my parents came from families with alcoholic fathers, my theory is that they drank excessively to numb the unresolved pain of their respective childhoods. In my view, drinking too much and smoking cigarettes caused their premature deaths, at ages fifty-nine and sixty-three.

2. **Venting and angry rants.** Some people are filled with rage about the hurt and harm they have sustained. One person I know seems angry all the time. She is frequently quite nasty in her communications. Her words are often offensive and off-putting. I've often wondered what happened to cause her to be filled with so much rage.

3. **Overeating and gluttony.** Another method of numbing pain is overeating. Food can become a kind of coping mechanism for people who have not found ways to reconcile or resolve issues with others from their past. They often gain a lot of weight, negatively impacting their overall health. The results are disastrous physically, mentally, emotionally, and spiritually.

4. **Feeling entitled and getting even.** Many victims of hurt and harm feel the world owes them for all they have endured in life. They feel they deserve to buy whatever they want as a means of payback. They feel entitled to everything life has to offer. In many cases, they run up enormous amounts of credit card debt buying things they don't need, then become imprisoned to paying huge sums of interest to credit card companies. It's all part of numbing their pain while they continue to withhold forgiveness.

5. **Being negative, dour, critical, and cantankerous.** Some angry folks seem to enjoy living with a chip on their shoulder. I once was joking with a cantankerous fellow I know, but he saw nothing funny about my humor. He retorted, "I beg your pardon?" in the nastiest tone I've ever heard. He lives with tremendous anger, which is evident to everyone around him.

6. **Going ballistic over minor life events.** When someone lives with underlying rage stemming from unfinished business about the pain they've experienced, that rage often erupts in inappropriate ways. They go nuts over minor life events and are easily annoyed, bothered, and aggravated by the small stuff of life.

When I encounter people like this, I often wonder, *What's going on inside this person? What causes this person to blow up so easily?* My theory is that they need to sort out exactly what is bothering them so much, and they need to do the hard work of resolving the issues of the past that are causing them to lose their cool in the present. Forgiving others and themselves is the remedy. This is hard work, but worth the effort.

For Reflection

1. In what ways might you be acting out in destructive or hurtful ways to help you numb the pain of past events?
2. What steps can you take to change this behavior?

CHAPTER 7

Coming to Our Senses

When we are willing to take a hard look at ourselves, we eventually begin to realize how much damage we are doing to ourselves by withholding forgiveness. By making an honest self-assessment, we come to truly understand that harboring of the poisons of unforgiveness are literally eating us alive.

Many years ago, I was driving down a freeway, talking on the phone to one of the individuals who had cheated me badly. I was suggesting ways he could pay me back. He scoffed at any of these suggestions, however, because he could never bring himself to admit to or confess his sins and wrongdoing toward me. I suddenly realized that I was never going to receive the apology I thought I was owed, nor was I going to be paid back the money I had earned and never received. I said to myself right then: "Thinking about this again for one second ever again is a complete and colossal waste of time!" This realization really helped me to move on from obsessing about this debacle in my life. From then on, I was able to finally let go of all the negative thoughts I'd carried for years; I no longer allowed them to bother me. This realization was the first step in finally being able to forgive this person.

Another important realization came to me. The Holy Spirit convicted me about my own wrongdoing in this failed relationship. To a large degree, I had brought a lot of the trauma on myself. Here's how:

- When I was warned by the Holy Spirit that there could be trouble in joining a certain company, I chose to ignore the warning.
- I joined this company because I was angry about another failed relationship. I felt that I had no choice. In reality, this was not true.
- I failed to get agreements in writing. I thought a verbal agreement and a handshake would be sufficient. I was very naïve.
- I did not examine the new firm closely enough. I quickly learned that the culture of the firm was not a good fit for my own value system.
- In reality, I forced my way into the firm because of what I saw as my needs at the time. What a huge mistake!

Eventually I came to realize that the person I had the most trouble forgiving was *me*. How could I have been so stupid? How could I have allowed myself to be taken advantage of so badly?

After some sober reflection on my own errors, I was able to seek the forgiveness of Our Lord. In so doing, I was able to finally forgive myself as well. Accepting God's forgiveness is an important step in this process. In Mark 2:5, Jesus says to the paralytic, "My child, your sins are forgiven." He says the same to us when we come to Him with contrite hearts, and He wants us to fully understand and accept that forgiveness so we can experience true freedom.

Here are some other important realizations in the forgiveness process:

- While harboring the poisons of unforgiveness, we ourselves are robbed of the joy of living in the Lord here and now.
- We remain distracted by past trauma and failed relationships.
- We might say to ourselves: "Enough is enough. I need to move on. I refuse to live this way any longer."
- We might be steeped in guilt, shame, and regret over how we contributed to the problems in prior relationships.

- The devil will dredge up the past. We need to take the authority Jesus has provided us and expel and rebuke the deceptions of the evil one.
- We come to the place where we can no longer ignore the poisons deep inside ourselves. They are eating us alive. Life is too short to live this way.
- We need to grapple with our unforgiveness, take steps to forgive and move on, and be set free. It's one of the best things we can ever do for ourselves!

For Reflection

1. In what ways are you coming to your senses about harboring unforgiveness in your life?
2. Have you looked soberly at the damage you are doing to yourself and others? What has this revealed to you?

CHAPTER 8

What Prevents Us from Wanting to Forgive?

Over the years, I've thought a lot about this question. Here are the major obstacles in forgiveness I have noticed in others, as well as for myself:

We demand an apology. We insist on the offender saying they are sorry for what they said or did. We want others to grovel and admit their wrongdoing. We want to see others squirm and feel the pain they have perpetrated upon us. We see this as the "condition" upon which we will base our forgiveness. We feel justified in withholding forgiveness until we receive an apology.

I like what Mother Teresa says: "People are illogical, self-centered and unreasonable. Forgive them anyway."

We want restitution. We can get cheated out of money in a myriad of ways. As another condition for forgiveness, we want every penny paid back to us, and we want it right now.

We are plotting revenge on our terms. We want to even the score, to retaliate, to exact revenge. We want others to experience every bit of the pain we felt. We want to tell others off, or even punch them out. Romans 12:19 offers great advice:

> Dear friends, never take revenge. Leave that to the righteous anger of God. For the Scriptures say, I will take revenge; I will pay them back, says the Lord.

Isn't it comforting to know that our Lord is dealing with the issue of revenge? Perhaps a better question for us is what we will say to defend ourselves when Our Lord is holding us accountable?

We replay our grievance story over and over. When we refuse to let go of what happened to us, it continues to occupy our minds with all the negativity of what happened. This rents way too much space in our minds. We remain distracted by the past.

What happened to us is unforgivable. Many people feel this way. They basically say, "I will never forgive this person for what they did—not on my watch!" But was the offense really unforgiveable?

We read the account of Jesus being crucified in Luke 23:32–43. Incredibly, in verse 34 Jesus says, "Father, forgive them, for they don't know what they are doing."

I dare say that the offenses against us generally pale in comparison to what Our Lord endured while being crucified on the Cross, and yet Jesus forgave the people who were murdering him.

Our pity party becomes our comfort zone. We might come to enjoy being a victim of the offenses of the past. We love having others feel sorry for us. This weird zone of comfort can be what we've come to know and how we live. We've forgotten or given up on trying to forgive others, and we relish living in our own misery. Again, it's just no way to live in Christ.

We "kick the can down the road." We assume that all the ravages of unforgiveness will just go away on their own. We buy into the myth that "time heals all wounds." In my experience, we have to grapple with what happened to us; these wounds do not disappear on their own.

Years ago, I prayed about finding a place to go when I felt despair or was imprisoned by the unresolved events of my past. The Lord led me to a place called the Healing Room, which is described in detail at EntertheHealingRoom.com. I invite you to check it out.

We blame God. We might rage against God and blame him for the hurt and harm we have sustained. I know; I've been there. I used to question God, saying, "Why did you allow all this bad stuff to happen to me? Where were you when all this was happening? What are you going to do about the offenders? Are you really going to allow this to happen again to someone else?"

You might have already surmised that God had nothing to do with allowing the sins of others to create hurt and harm in us. He is not to blame. Our Lord is weeping with us over the hurtful sins of others. He is ready to help us pick up the pieces, and He wants to set us free.

We tell ourselves, "I'll figure this out on my own." For way too long, my internal voice told me I could sort out all my forgiveness problems on my own. I refused to ask Jesus for help, and instead continued replaying my grievance stories. It was "Woe is me," or "I'll get to all this later." My experience has shown me that true forgiveness doesn't happen without the power and inspiration of Our Lord and His Holy Spirit. The real turning point in my case happened just a few years ago, when I finally surrendered my stubborn will and asked for help from our dear Lord and Savior. He has been with me every step of the way. Jesus is inviting all of us to seek His help in becoming set free.

We cannot forgive ourselves. We may have contributed to the problems we've had with others. We may have fanned the flame of discord, animosity, and hostility. We may have made bad decisions or reacted badly ourselves. We may be stuck in guilt, shame, and regret for what we did or did not do.

I love the words of Paul in Romans 8:1—"So now there is no condemnation for those who belong to Christ Jesus."

In the end, we might have the most trouble forgiving ourselves for our past sins and mistakes. When we truly accept our Lord's forgiveness, though, we are in a far better spot to forgive the wrongdoing of others.

We are steeped in self-righteous indignation. Our own ego and pride might be in the way of forgiveness. We might believe that forgiving others renders us the loser—that the offender will have won the battle. Nothing could be further from the truth. In forgiving, we are the winners. In forgiving, we become more and more like Christ.

We refuse to reconcile. As Christians, we should be the first ones to reach out to attempt to resolve issues and reconcile with our offenders. Instead, we might tend to wait for the other person to reach out first. There are family members who refuse to speak with or be in the presence of other family members. In many cases, this is due to minor spats or disagreements. Things get blown out of proportion, and a molehill suddenly becomes a mountain of resentment, bitterness, and blame. How sad!

It's crucial for us to figure out what is preventing us from forgiving others—or ourselves. This takes courage and a lot of self-effacing honesty. Such a rigorous assessment of ourselves isn't much fun; however, many blessings are in store for us if we do it. In my own life, assessing all the above points has been very helpful to me in moving on from the ravages of unforgiveness.

For Reflection

1. What are your biggest roadblocks in wanting to forgive?
2. In what ways might you be too callous or too hard-hearted? Ask Jesus to help you learn His ways of forgiveness.

CHAPTER 9

What Does Jesus Want to Teach Us?

In the Scriptures, Jesus devotes a lot of attention to forgiveness. In the Bible I use, there are more than 50 references to the topic of forgiveness. I think it's good for us to study these Scriptures on forgiveness. Jesus wants to teach us about forgiveness, because He knows the damage we can do to ourselves and others when we don't forgive. The following bullet points provide a good starting point.

- Matthew 6:14-15 tells us that if we refuse to forgive others, God cannot forgive our sins. In my own life, I have frequently forgotten about these verses. I was intent on judging, or plotting revenge, or bad-mouthing my former offenders. These verses should always be right in front of us on our path to forgiveness.
- Our Lord reminds us that harboring the poisons of unforgiveness can destroy our well-being and adversely affect our physical, mental, emotional, and spiritual health. Hebrews 12:15 says: "Look after each other so that none of you fails to receive the grace of God. Watch out that no poisonous root of bitterness grows up to trouble you, corrupting many."
- Jesus desires for us to be set free. When we harbor unforgiveness in our hearts and minds, it's a bit like dragging around a huge bag of rocks everywhere we go. Jesus invites us to drop that bag of rocks today. Jesus wants to free us from all bondage, strongholds, fixations, and burdens. He wants to restore our

well-being. We cannot truly live for Jesus or be effective in serving others if we are still stuck in unforgiveness.
- Jesus asks us to repent of all our own wrongdoing and sins in our relationships with others, including judgments, condemnations, bad-mouthing, gossip, slander, hatred, the desire for revenge, and harboring grudges, resentment, and bitterness. 1 John 1:8–10 speaks well to these kinds of sins:

> If we claim we have no sin, we are only fooling ourselves and not living in the truth. But if we confess our sins to him, he is faithful and just to forgive us our sins and to cleanse us from all wickedness. If we claim we have not sinned, we are calling God a liar and showing that his word has no place in our hearts.

In my view, confessing our wrongdoing can take place in at least three ways:

1. We can confess and admit our sins to God, who is always willing to forgive us. Jesus is our Redeemer and Sanctifier.
2. We can attend a reconciliation conversation with a member of the clergy. In the Catholic Church, there is the Sacrament of Reconciliation, an opportunity for honestly admitting our sins, and then receiving good instructions on how to avoid these in the future.
3. We can seek forgiveness from the person who offended us for bad-mouthing them and being judgmental. Some powerful words are: "I owe you an apology. Will you forgive me?"

In Luke 5:20, Jesus said to a man: "Young man, your sins are forgiven." In the middle of our struggles to forgive others (or ourselves), we might justify or rationalize our sinful thoughts or behaviors. We can bellow: "But they wronged me!" We have to remember that our judgments against others are sins before God. If we confess and own up to our sins, our loving Lord will forgive us.

Jesus wants to teach us about His amazing love for others and ourselves. In fact, in Matthew 5:43–48, Jesus challenges us to love our enemies— the very people who have created so much harm and hurt in our lives.

> "If you love only those who love you, what reward is there for that? Even corrupt tax collectors do that much. If you are kind only to your friends, how are you different from anyone else? Even pagans do that. But you are to be perfect (mature), even as your Father in heaven is perfect."

Loving the people who have harmed us is a challenging call. We all have difficult people around us. We can imagine Jesus's heart of love for all people and ask Him to fill us with that love.

Jesus Wants to Deliver Us from Bondage

We can feel imprisoned and trapped by our unforgiveness. We may feel hopeless and helpless. We are not sure what to do or where to go. The devil loves for us to be in this predicament. The evil one wants to deceive us into thinking we cannot or never will forgive certain people. The evil one tempts us to never forgive anyone ever.

Deliverance has to do with being set free by rebuking and expelling the tactics of the devil. We can only do so in the name of Jesus. Our Lord has given us the authority to expel demons and all influences of evil. Whenever we feel we are being attacked, we can start a prayer with "In the name of Jesus" and expel and rebuke all evil spirits. We tell them to leave, and we order them to stay away from us. In the sovereign power of Jesus, they leave. However, these evil spirits will always try to return by "dredging up the past"; they try to create doubt about whether we have ever truly forgiven anyone. We learn more about this in chapter 11.

Filled with the Fruit of the Holy Spirit

An excellent barometer for us in our forgiveness journey is how well we are living out the fruit of the Holy Spirit: love, joy, peace, patience, kindness, gentleness, goodness, faithfulness and self-control (see Galatians 5:22–23). We can test this as we think about our most challenging relationships in life. How are we doing with loving an annoying person? What about being kind to someone we find offensive? What about mustering self-control when we are tempted to retaliate in kind with mean words? Could we be more patient with certain people?

I was praying the other day about a person who attends the church we attend. I find this person annoying. I know we all go about life in very different ways. As I thought about why I find this person so bothersome, I came to realize that seeing this person at their worst often reminds me a lot of me at my worst. This realization has helped me to cut this person some slack and be reminded of the ways I could be offensive to others as well. It's moved me a lot closer to forgiving this person.

Filled with the fruit of the Holy Spirit, we have the power to become "automatic forgivers." Philippians 4:8–9 talks about "putting into practice the Christlike things we have seen and heard." We can get better at forgiving others and ourselves. We become less thin-skinned, less bothered by the words and actions of others. It takes a lot for us to become angry, annoyed, or aggravated with others. We practice the tools of restraint when tempted to respond in kind. The call to forgive seventy times seven in Matthew 18:21–22 becomes easier and easier through constant practice.

For Reflection

1. What is Jesus teaching you about forgiveness?
2. What new ideas and approaches to forgiveness are you open to?

CHAPTER 10

Studying the Scriptures

Studying God's Word has been a real game changer for me in learning about the call to forgive and in being empowered to forgive. Jesus offers us great advice and direct challenges to forgive. He IS the greatest example for knowing how to forgive. Imagine this: While being crucified, he asks the Father to forgive His murderers because "they don't know what they are doing" (Luke 23:34). Learning about these Scriptures has enabled me to lean on them constantly, especially when I'm dealing with a difficult person.

One of the core forgiveness Scriptures is in Matthew 7:1-5. The essence of these verses is DO NOT JUDGE. We are to take the log out of our own eye before judging and condemning others. Talk about putting forgiveness into practice!

Here are several of my go-to Scriptures that have provided tremendous help to me in the forgiveness and healing process:

- **Matthew 6:14–15** says that our Father cannot forgive us for our sins if we do not forgive the sins of others. Over many years, I either ignored or forgot these words. These words are crucially important.
- **John 8:1–11** is the story of a woman caught in adultery, who is about to be stoned to death by the legalists of the day. Then Jesus says: "Let the one who has never sinned throw the first

stone!" Once the elders heard these words, they walked away one by one, realizing they had no right to judge or condemn anyone. They remembered that they too were filled with sin.
- **Ephesians 4:31–32** says, "Get rid of all bitterness, rage, anger, harsh words, and slander, as well as all types of evil behavior. Instead, be kind to each other, tenderhearted, forgiving one another, just as God through Christ has forgiven you." This pretty much says it all in just a few verses.
- **Luke 11:4** issues a strong call to forgive others. "Forgive us our sins, as we forgive those who sin against us." This is from the Lord's Prayer. It's simple and full of meaning.
- **Matthew 5:38–42** calls us to NOT retaliate when others sin against us—no more of the eye-for-an-eye exacting revenge. Instead, Jesus calls us to turn the other cheek. "If you are sued in court and your shirt is taken from you, give your coat, too. Give to those who ask, and don't turn away from those who want to borrow." Jesus calls us not to keep score, but to love and forgive. These words are 180 degrees from the ways the world handles issues with others. We should study them closely.
- **Matthew 5:43–48** tells us to love our enemies. What? Jesus calls us to LOVE our enemies? When I first learned about these verses, my first reaction was: "Are you out of your mind? Don't you know what they did to me? How can I love my enemies?" I see these challenging verses as some of the toughest ones to follow in all of the Bible. These verses have caused me to at least try to understand the people I regard as enemies. Fortunately, I have very few (if any) real enemies in my own life. I've tried to replace my former judgments and condemnation with mercy and compassion.
- **Romans 12:17–19** says, "Never pay back evil with more evil. Do things in such a way that everyone can see you are honorable. Do all you can to live in peace with everyone. Dear friends, never take revenge. Leave that to the righteous anger of God. For the Scriptures say, 'I will take revenge: I will pay them back,' says the Lord." As I learned more about God's ways

through the Scriptures, I was greatly relieved to know that ALL offenders will have to account for their own lives. Since God is handling revenge, we don't have to. What a relief! God will deal with all of us in His timing, and in His ways.

- **Matthew 18:21–22** is an eye-opener. "Then Peter came to him (Jesus) and asked, 'Lord how often should I forgive someone who sins against me? Seven times?' 'No, not seven times,' Jesus replied, 'but seventy times seven!'" Incredible, right? We are called to *unlimited* amounts of forgiveness. We should not keep track of how many times we forgive. We should always forgive those who are truly repentant, no matter how many times they ask.

I've often wondered about the offenders in our lives who are not repentant. Does the "seventy times seven" rule apply here too? What about the truly obnoxious, loudmouth in our midst who is offensive and oblivious to his or her actions? In these cases, I've reflected on one of the Spiritual Works of Mercy of the Catholic Church: to admonish sinners. I don't believe we are called to be doormats for continued bad behavior. Sometimes we need to call people out for their offensive actions. But we should do so with great gentleness and love.

- **Leviticus 19:17–18** is very clear. "Do not nurse hatred in your heart for any of your relatives. Confront people directly so you will not be held guilty for their sin. Do not seek revenge or bear a grudge against a fellow Israelite, but love your neighbor as yourself. I am the Lord."
- **Ezekiel 36:25–27** are verses full of hope and a promise from God. "I will give you a new heart, and I will put a new spirit in you. I will take out your stony, stubborn heart and give you a tender, responsive heart." In my experience, true forgiveness comes from our hearts and minds. It's common while harboring unforgiveness to be hard-hearted, stubborn, and refusing to forgive. We are called to replace this stony heart

with tenderhearted mercy—just like the mercy Our Lord has poured out on us.

- **1 Peter 5:8–9** says, "Stay alert! Watch out for your great enemy, the devil. He prowls around like a roaring lion, looking for someone to devour. Stand firm against him, and be strong in your faith."
- **1 Corinthians 13:4–7** tells us: "Love is patient and kind. Love is not jealous or boastful or proud or rude. It does not demand its own way. It is not irritable, and keeps no record of being wronged. It does not rejoice about injustice but rejoices whenever the truth wins out. Love never gives up, never loses faith, is always hopeful, and endures through every circumstance."

These verses can surely apply to our call to forgive others. Yes! We are called to even love our offenders.

- **Luke 7:47–48** says, "'I tell you, her sins—and they are many—have been forgiven, so she has shown me much love. But a person who is forgiven little shows only little love.' Then Jesus said to the woman, 'Your sins are forgiven.'"

Only those who fully comprehend the depth of their own sin can appreciate the complete forgiveness God offers to us. I have been riveted by these words: "But a person who is forgiven little shows only little love." Jesus has rescued all of us from eternal death. Do we truly appreciate the wideness of His mercy? Are we truly grateful for His forgiveness?

- **Matthew 11:28–30** is an invitation to rest from the burden of unforgiveness. "Then Jesus said, "Come to me, all of you who are weary and carry heavy burdens, and I will give you rest. Take my yoke upon you. Let me teach you, because I am humble and gentle at heart, and you will find rest for your souls. For my yoke is easy to bear, and the burden I give you is light." After many years of suffering in unforgiveness, I finally came to an acute realization: I was only creating damage to myself by

- harboring grudges, resentments, unforgiveness, bitterness, and blame against the people who harmed me. I needed to "entrust my wounds" to Jesus, the Great Healer, the Great Physician. I needed to surrender my offenders to Jesus. I was way out of my element on my own. I needed to hand all my burdens and bondage to our loving Lord. He, of course, fully took them from me. He has provided His Sovereign graces and healing to me in the process. He has set me free.
- **Colossians 3:12–15** captures so well our call in Christ regarding forgiveness. "Since God chose you to be the holy people he loves, you must clothe yourselves with tenderhearted mercy, kindness, humility, gentleness, and patience. Make allowance for each other's faults, and forgive anyone who offends you. Remember, the Lord forgave you, so you must forgive others. Above all, clothe yourselves with love, which binds us all together in perfect harmony. And let the peace that comes from Christ rule in your hearts. For as members of one body you are called to live in peace. And always be thankful." If I had to point anyone to ONE Scripture on forgiveness, this would be the one. It tells us exactly what to do.

The above-mentioned verses have helped me greatly in my own journey in forgiveness. I've come to love the study of these verses to:

- Assess how I'm doing in my struggles to forgive
- Teach me new ways to go about forgiving
- See examples of Christ himself exercising forgiveness
- Come under Christ's Lordship when I'm refusing to forgive
- Change from judgments and condemnations to mercy and compassion
- Be reminded about what I am being called to do in His power

For Reflection:

1. As you study these Scriptures, ask: What is Jesus wanting to teach me in these verses? How do they apply to me? How can they help to heal me?
2. What will you begin to do today to exercise forgiveness in your own life?
3. Which Scriptures really stand out as most effective to you? Write them in your journal and reflect on them regularly.

CHAPTER 11

Deliverance from the Bondage of Evil Spirits

We need to realize that we are under attack from the evil one, especially when we are doing the hard work of forgiving others or ourselves. We must not be naïve about Satan's tactics. The devil will pull out all the stops to prevent forgiveness, because the evil one knows this is exactly what Jesus desires for us—and the evil one HATES Jesus.

> Stay alert! Watch out for your great enemy, the devil. He prowls around looking for someone to devour. Stand firm against him, and be strong in your faith. Remember that your family of believers all over the world are going through the same kind of suffering you are. (1 Peter 5:8–9)

From years of experience in dealing with forgiveness issues, I have concluded that:

- The devil doesn't want us to forgive anyone and will go to great lengths to attempt to prevent us from forgiving others—or ourselves.
- The devil will plant seeds of doubt about whether we have actually forgiven others, when in fact we have.
- The devil will dredge up the past and tempt us again into judgment and contempt for our offenders.

- We have been given the authority of Jesus to rebuke and expel the evil one and his demons, by praying a simple prayer beginning with "In the name of Jesus . . ." The evil one hates that name and is powerless when it is invoked. Remember, though, the evil spirits will leave, but they will try to return.
- James 4:7–10 is a powerful set of verses to help us in dealing with evil spirits.
- We need to put on the armor of God described in Ephesians 6:10–20.
- In very serious cases, we may need clergy who are trained in dealing with the devil, to be delivered from the bondage of evil spirits.

Several years ago, I was being trained to pray with people for healing at a Healing Room in San Clemente, California. We were asked to arrive one hour early to spend time in praise and worship and be anointed with holy oil in preparation for praying with others. The leader asked us, "Do you know what we call this room?" None of us knew the answer. He then said, "We call this the War Room. Today, you will be engaged in spiritual warfare!" And it was true—the people we prayed with did have many problems, troubles, strongholds, fixations, roadblocks, defiance. The devil was at work.

All of my research and study on forgiveness, as well as my personal experiences, have led me to the conclusion that the devil will do everything possible to prevent any of us from having a desire to forgive. This IS spiritual warfare!

Let's get familiar with some of the devil's tactics in preventing forgiveness.

1. He tempts us to continue to judge and condemn our offenders. We continue to bad-mouth others behind their backs with gossip and slander.
2. He dupes us into hating other people or ourselves. He wants us to wish others were dead.

3. He dredges up the past, trying to convince us that we have not forgiven anyone, when in fact we have.
4. He stirs up anger and seething rage in us. We lose our tempers a lot, and over minor issues.
5. He tricks us into believing that "nothing happened," when in fact we have suffered devastating hurt and harm.
6. He convinces us that we can "figure out" this forgiveness work on our own without the help of Jesus.
7. He plants vile explosions of rage within us, resulting in loud, ugly, and profane rants that "pop out" from nowhere.
8. He loves for us to replay our grievance stories over and over again. We tell our story to anyone within earshot.
9. He directs us into "victimhood." We live in a perpetual pity party. We insist on asking, "Don't you want to feel sorry for me?"
10. He wants us to be STUCK in unforgiveness for the rest of our lives. We experience constant despair, dourness, despondency, or even depression.
11. He wants us to refuse to forgive out of self-righteous indignation. We were right. How dare this other person say or do what they did to me?
12. He lures us into harboring, grudges, resentments, bitterness and blame.
13. He tempts us to numb our pain with alcohol, drugs, porn, or gluttony.
14. He wants us to refuse to apologize for our own wrongdoing. Although we have caused dissension ourselves, we will not reach out to reconcile.
15. He wants us to remain agitated, short, rude, irascible, nasty, or even vicious with others.
16. He doesn't want us to tolerate anything resembling constructive criticism.

For we are not fighting against flesh-and-blood enemies, but against evil rulers and authorities of the unseen world, against mighty powers in this dark world, and against evil spirits in the heavenly places. (Ephesians 6:12)

Do I think the devil is at the bottom of every one of these issues all the time? I do not. We should not give the devil credit for all the problems we encounter. We humans are complicated and can get swept up in our emotions at times. We just have to be aware of the relentless tricks and tactics of the devil. For example, it's a sign that the devil is at work if:

- We want to blast someone and respond in kind
- We get very angry over minor events
- We continue to judge and condemn others harshly
- We refuse to consider forgiveness, because what someone did was "unforgiveable"
- We vow to never forgive an offender
- We continue to allow ourselves to be the "victim"

We Are Well-Equipped

What are our weapons in RESPONSE to the attacks of the evil one? The Scriptures tell us we are well-equipped to deal with the devil's antics and tactics.

- For the word of God is alive and powerful. It is sharper than the sharpest two-edged sword, cutting between soul and spirit, between joint and marrow. It exposes our innermost thoughts and desires. Nothing in all creation is hidden from God. Everything is naked and exposed before his eyes, and he is the one to whom we are accountable. (Hebrews 4:12–13)
- For he has rescued us from the kingdom of darkness and transferred us into the Kingdom of his dear Son, who purchased our freedom and forgave our sins. (Colossians 1:13–14)
- We are human, but we don't wage war as humans do. We use God's mighty weapons, not worldly weapons, to knock down the strongholds of human reasoning and to destroy false arguments. We destroy every proud obstacle that keeps people from knowing God. We capture their rebellious thoughts and teach them to obey Christ. (2 Corinthians 10:3–5)

Good News!

Let's look at the authority Jesus has given us to renounce, rebuke, and expel demons and evil spirits. Several Scriptures describe the powers Jesus has provided us to banish demons: Matthew 28:18-20; Matthew 10:1; Mark 3:15; Mark 6:7. Jesus gave his disciples and apostles these powers, and we are his modern-day disciples. We can invoke these powers anytime through prayer.

Here is a powerful prayer I've used over many years when I sense I'm under attack from evil spirits:

> In the name of Jesus, I come against all the tactics of the devil. I renounce, rebuke and expel any demons of anger, judgments, hatred, fear, held grudges, resentments, unforgiveness, bitterness, blame, or anything which is not of your Perfect Design and Will for me. I take authority against all these demons in Your Most Holy and Precious Name. I command all these demons to leave right now, and stay away from me. In Your Name Lord Jesus! Amen.

You can pray this prayer together with anyone who is struggling with unforgiveness and you suspect the person is under attack. Two or more people using this prayer invites even more of Christ's power in healing.

Another important Scripture that can assist us in expelling demons is found in James 4:7–10:

> So humble yourselves before God. Resist the devil, and he will flee from you. Come close to God, and he will come close to you. Wash your hands, you sinners; purify your hearts, for your loyalty is divided between God and the world.(Stuck in unforgiveness.) Let there be tears for what you have done. Let there be sorrow and deep grief. Let there be sadness instead of laughter, and gloom

instead of joy. Humble yourselves before the Lord, and he will lift you up in honor.

I discovered a great prayer through a helpful series, *How to Forgive*.[4] It's called a Deliverance Prayer for Unforgiveness:

> Lord Jesus Christ, I am truly sorry for any sins I have committed in allowing Satan, any evil spirits, any lies of the devil, or any false vows into my heart, my family, or any endeavor.
>
> I forgive everyone who has harmed me, and I forgive myself for my sins. I accept your forgiveness, and through the blood of Jesus Christ, and by the power of his Holy Cross, I command you evil spirits, all companion spirits, all false vows and all the lies of the devil to be bound and broken, and go to the foot of the Cross for Jesus to deal with as He wills.
>
> Come Holy Spirit! Fill me with your peace, love, joy, healing grace, strength, power and holy purity. Amen.

For Reflection

1. Do you believe that evil exists?
2. Are you under attack right now? Describe how you are feeling and then pray the powerful prayer found in the Good News section of this chapter.
3. What might you do differently in the future when you sense an attack from evil spirits?

---

[4] https://www.goodcatholic.com/product/how-to-forgive/.

CHAPTER 12

Tools and Resources for Forgiving Others

In recent years, I've thought a lot about the process of forgiving. What do we actually do? What happens? How do we forgive? How do we move on in life?

The following ideas are all ones I have incorporated into my own journey. I hope you will find a few which will work for you too.

Lean on Jesus

A key ingredient in my personal forgiveness journey has been increasing reliance and trust in our loving Lord to assist me. I'm convinced that we need His supernatural powers and grace to forgive and move on in life and be set free. Healing is always inspired by the Holy Spirit.

For way too long, I resisted enlisting Jesus's help in my forgiveness struggles. I figured (wrongly) that my pain would just go away on its own. I figured I could sort out what to do to get an apology, restitution, and revenge. I decided I didn't need His help. I can tell you now that the biggest regret of my life has been the amount of time and energy I have exerted on the worthless pursuit of getting even or trying to "settle the score." I needed to let go and move on far sooner. What a giant waste of time and energy!

Some years ago, I had a vision of Jesus sitting on a throne of grace. He sat on an elegant chair in a large room, His pure white robes draped all around Him. There were some steps to walk up to meet Him. He had His arms and hands outstretched to me, and without any words, he invited me to place any and all of my burdens right in His hands. All my struggles just disappeared instantly. The burdens were all gone! I immediately felt relieved and freed up from years of carrying this weight around in my body, mind, and soul.

In the course of thinking deeply about my own struggles in forgiveness, I have grown far closer to Jesus. We are good friends. Nothing is held back. I constantly am reminded about who I'm called to be in Him—especially forgiving as He forgives. "In him, we live and move and have our being. (Acts 17:28).

While Our Lord was being crucified on the Cross, in excruciating pain, He was still able to ask His Father to forgive his tormentors (see Luke 23:34). Whatever pain we might be feeling from others in our own lives is nothing compared to the pain He endured for us on the Cross.

A while back, I had a conversation with Jesus about my forgiveness process. I found His words to be very encouraging. I think they are meant for all of us:

> Thanks for inviting Me to help you with the difficult and challenging people you have encountered and will encounter in your lives. I know the pain you have endured. I experienced this very same pain when I was here in human form on this earth.
>
> I'm aware of what happened to you and why it happened. I was present in every aspect of the bad treatment, the harsh words, the ugly behavior, the arguments and fighting. I watched as others sinned against you. None of these were caused by me.

The people who offended you are also my children. Many are lost in the ways of this sinful world. Many "knew not what they were doing." I pray they will make amends with you and attempt to find reconciliation and healing with you. Please continue to pray and intercede for them yourselves. This proves your love and commitment to Me as your Lord and Savior.

Continue to come to Me amid your own hurts and wounds from the past, or for whatever may be happening right now. My hands and arms are outstretched to you. Abide in and trust in Me. Continue the hard work of forgiving, and I will provide you with My help. I will deliver you from all bondage of any kind and set you free.

Personal Prayer and Journaling

I am committed to personal daily prayer. Christians in Commerce (now Worklight.org) calls this an "appointment with God." And since I'm a note taker and like writing things down, journaling has been crucially important in my own forgiveness journey. My journals are 8.5" by 11" and the paper I use is three-hole punched. I'm constantly writing notes and questions in my time with the Lord. This helps me to process things quickly, always with the question in mind: "Lord, what are you trying to teach me today?"

For my prayer and journaling time, I like early mornings the best. It's quiet and I have dedicated time to be with the Lord before doing anything else. I use a prayer format known as ACTS (adoration, contrition, thanksgiving, and supplication). I try to include each of these in my daily prayers.

I use a good study Bible. Study Bibles are important for looking up key Scriptures with commentaries. I have looked up key Scriptures on forgiveness, mercy, compassion, deliverance, healing, love, etc. A concordance for looking up Scriptures is another valuable resource for studying God's Word on any topic.

Periodically, I wake up in a foul mood. I might be angry with someone or annoyed about something. During my prayer time, I write down how I'm feeling. I transfer whatever rage in me on to the page. Yes, Our Lord allows us to vent a bit in our time with Him. In my conversations with Him on these days, He reminds me about who I am called to be. As I realize what is happening, Our Lord calms me down. I never leave those times of prayer in an angry state of mind.

My quiet time with Jesus has been a game changer for me when it comes to forgiving others and myself. The benefits include:

- Being able to vent and be completely honest with Our Lord
- Writing out my feelings, both positive and negative
- Being very conscious of Christ's call to forgive
- Immersing myself in the Bible, which provides wisdom and guidance
- Growing in mercy, compassion, and understanding
- Emulating the love Jesus has for me to others
- Being empowered to act through the Holy Spirit
- Growing closer to Jesus in every area of my life

The Vent Letter Process

This forgiveness strategy has five steps. The Lord gave me this to me as a regular "go-to" process when I find myself struggling with others.

Step 1: Write down what happened. What caused you to be offended, wounded, damaged, or hurt? Record characteristics about the offender such as *control freak, angry, wounded, hurt, egotist, arrogant, insensitive, incompetent, glad-handing bigmouth*, etc. Let it fly onto the paper in front of you. Transfer whatever rage you are feeling onto to the page. In my mind, it's OK to vent and judge and rant a bit because, this paper is ONLY for you. You are not sending this to anyone. You may choose to share it with a close trusted friend; however, it's basically for you alone. Writing down your feelings and emotions is therapeutic. It removes the toxic poisons away from you and onto the paper. You have the entire situation right in front of you. You'll often realize that you've made a bigger deal out of certain conflicts than you needed to—you've made a mountain out of a molehill. Pray about what is right in front of you. Ask: Lord, what are you trying to teach me here?"

Step 2: Ask yourself some tough questions. *How did I goof up? What mistakes did I make? Did I in some ways add to the problems in a difficult relationship by trying to force, compel others or get my own way? Was I rude, short, defensive, or irritable? Did I somehow fan the flame of even deeper discord, animosity, or hostility? Was I too harsh?*

It's very possible that we have done nothing wrong ourselves. The child who was abused or heavily criticized has done nothing wrong. But in many situations, you may have contributed to the issues that arise in your relationships, and as you answer these questions, you might realize that you have to take responsibility for what's occurred.

Step 3: Write what you've learned. Take some time to document the lessons gained in the midst of a challenging relationship or situation. What "emotional tuition" have you paid? Some of my takeaways include:

- Some people are really different from me. We don't always agree on things.
- Some live in an altered reality that I do not understand. Some people act badly for their own reasons. In most cases, I'll never know the reasons.
- I tend to have problems with control freaks. Maybe it's because I'm looking in the mirror when I see them?
- Hurt people hurt people. I need to pray for those who hurt me—and help them if I can.
- I need to try to understand others, rather than judge and condemn them.

- I'm called to be filled with the fruit of the Holy Spirit (see Galatians 5:22–23), especially patience, kindness, gentleness, and self-control.
- In many cases, I was too "thin-skinned" and took things way too personally.

Step 4: List some things you are grateful for. Are you grateful for all that has happened? How can you be grateful for hurts and harm which come your way? While coming under the Lordship of Jesus Christ, you recognize the growth you can experience in seeking and receiving His enormous help in forgiveness. You grow in trust and friendship with the Lord, fully knowing that He is with you in all the tough stuff of life. I look back now at all the scrapes, skirmishes, arguments, and difficulties I've encountered with others; Our Lord has gotten me through every single one of them. He has protected, provided, and guided me. His love has been amazing. His power to help us is amazing.

Step 5: Consider the next steps. What's next in your broken relationships? What are the opportunities now? Write out some possible actions you might take. If nothing seems to occur to you, at least continue to pray for these relationships.

A common benefit of this vent letter process is the reminder to judge and condemn less, and instead to muster mercy and compassion for others. Another benefit is looking for the good in others. All people have goodness and dignity. Everyone is a child of God, so how can we be lights to others who do not yet know God?

The vast majority of my own offenders are not yet believers in Christ. I can do all I can to invite them into the bounty of living in the Lord. Imagine being transformed from grudges, hatred, resentments, bitterness, anger, and unforgiveness to actually pray for and intercede on behalf of the offenders in my midst. It's God's saving grace at work!

Reconcile for Closure

> Reconciliation requires a considerable measure of humility—not belittling ourselves, but about seeing ourselves honestly—faults, strengths, errors (sins), and right actions all together—and being able to admit our failings toward another with a willingness to seek forgiveness. Humility combined with love is powerful. It knocks down barriers (strongholds) among us and opens the door to reconciliation and unity. (Louis Grams, founder of Christians in Commerce)[5]

Ideally, we'd have a calm conversation with a person with whom we have had problems. It's important to pray for peace and humility before these kinds of meetings. An honest description of what happened can occur, if both parties are willing. I've enjoyed seeing the real fruit and blessings of these kinds of conversations. They help to resolve issues. Genuine apologies can happen. Friendships can be restored. The hatchet can be buried.

In one situation, I was wrongly accused of something and became the scapegoat for my manager. I was told to "turn in my keys by Friday." Fortunately, I did not have to leave that Friday, but the situation bothered me for several months. I was leaving this company anyway, but if I'd been forced to leave early, it would have created a lot of turmoil I did not need at the time.

After several months, I requested a lunch meeting with the manager. I simply wanted to understand what had happened and why I had been singled out. I was still put out by the prior events. At that lunch, I honestly and directly shared my concerns. Suddenly, the manager reached her hand across the table and said she was sorry. I could see that it was a genuine and heartfelt apology. All the tension, anger, and anxiety I had been carrying around disappeared in that moment and never returned. The relationship was restored.

---

[5] Taken from a *Christians in Commerce* newsletter.

In another situation, I'd had ongoing troubles for a few years with another Christian. He and I were very different in style, approach, focus, and methods. I think we both liked having control; however, I eventually looked back and realized my own errors in the relationship. I called him one day and said, "Joe [not his real name], I was very hard on you. I owe you an apology. Could you forgive me?" We only spoke that day for about ten minutes, but it was the best conversation we'd ever had. That relationship was healed during that phone call.

In Luke 15:11–32, we read the story of the Prodigal Son. To me, this is one of the best stories of reconciliation of all time. In this story, the youngest son in a Jewish family demands his inheritance early, before his father's death. In that culture, this was not done. This was beyond rude and insensitive. The father kindly grants the son's wish, and he goes off to waste his inheritance on wine, women, and song in a foreign country. After spending all his inheritance, the son finds himself in a pig pit feeding pigs, something highly against the rules of his Jewish heritage. He finally "comes to his senses," realizing that he'd be far better off as a lowly worker on his father's ranch. The father, who has been praying for the return of his lost son, sees him one day on the horizon as the son is heading home. The father is overjoyed and orders the fatted calf to be prepared for a huge celebration. His lost son had returned, and he welcomes him home with open arms!

Six Steps to Unlocking Forgiveness[6]

1. Find a good friend or mentor you trust to pray with you. Ideally, this person will be mature and is a person who has struggled with and has overcome forgiveness issues in their own lives. You need to feel safe with this person.
2. Begin to praise God and thank him. Psalms 145—150 are all psalms of praise. You can use any portions of these. For instance:

---

[6] I'm borrowing and paraphrasing from six recommended steps from Neal Lozano's book *Unbound: A Practical Guide to Deliverance* (Grand Rapids, MI: Chosen Books, 2010), which I believe are very effective.

"Enter his gates with thanksgiving; go into his courts with praise" (Psalm 100:4). Your adoration of Our Lord indicates that you know God is God, and you acknowledge His power in helping you with tough tasks.

3. When you sense His presence, you are delighted that Jesus is the author and perfecter of your faith. You acknowledge His amazing love and power for you. As believers who belong to Him, we identify with Him in every aspect of our lives. The Holy Spirit lives in us. When we hold back forgiveness, we have not surrendered to the One who loves us. Pray out loud: "Lord Jesus, please forgive me for trying to save my own life, for not relying on You, for not trusting You."

4. Remember the words of Jesus on the Cross: "Father, forgive them—they know not what they are doing" (Luke 23:34). These are eternal words that our Lord has given to us. When others hurt us, they may have been operating in an altered reality, which was certainly not Christlike.

5. Think of the person who hurt you, and what that person did. Allow yourself to feel that pain. Forgiveness takes a deeper hold on us when we forgive from a place of pain. Once you are in touch with the pain, you can say out loud: In the name of Jesus, I forgive_____ for_____. In my own life, I thought of being cheated, betrayed, criticized and not supported by a particular person. I remembered how he denied all wrongdoing and was a really bad example of how a Christian person is supposed to live. These were the specific areas I then forgave this person for. Saying all this **out loud** helps in two good ways:

- ✓ It helps us focus on specifics and keeps us from being vague.
- ✓ We can listen to ourselves to see if we are being genuine. Are we just mouthing the words, or are we really forgiving this person?

Have the friend pray with you that the love of God would release you and make you a vessel of His love. Repeat these steps if others you need to forgive come to mind.

If you have trouble speaking declarations of forgiveness, try speaking to the Lord about your hurt and pain. Let Him lead you to a place of forgiveness.

6. Give thanks to God for His goodness, and ask Him to direct your paths. Use your newfound freedom to love others in practical ways. The fruit of forgiveness is love. We can learn to love our offenders.

A wonderful story of forgiveness is portrayed in the movie *A Beautiful Day in the Neighborhood*, which tells the story of TV star Mr. Rogers, played by Tom Hanks. A reporter (Matthew Rhys) is asked to do a story about Mr. Rogers for *Esquire* magazine. What gets revealed is the high level of resentment and bitterness that this reporter has for his own awful father (Chris Cooper.) In interviewing Mr. Rogers, who encourages acceptance and forgiveness of everyone, this reporter is able to come to terms with the issues in his own life. It's a touching story about becoming aware of the issues in unforgiveness, then learning to move on.

A Word about Incompatibility

We tend to make the assumption that we should be able to get along with everyone we meet. I've come to learn that compatibility with others isn't always possible. No two humans are alike, and I've surely had my differences with more than a few people.

Incompatibility with certain people is unfortunate, but it's not a crime. I've just learned that it's better to stay away from certain people, with whom I have very little in common and no chemistry whatsoever. Some of these relationships can be toxic—especially with people who have harmed us. However, our call from Jesus is to forgive anyway and love our enemies (see Matthew 5:43–48).

People have very different personalities, styles, approaches, priorities, and ways of being. Some of these might be very bothersome to us, or even make us angry. I've gotten better at looking for the good in others, listening more intently, and disagreeing politely if necessary.

A sure test for me with incompatible folks is my willingness to judge less and pray and intercede for them more. Differences are OK. Oswald Chambers says that our most important job as a Christian is to pray and intercede for others, and our enemies (and the people with whom we are incompatible) should be at the top of the list.

A fabulous example of overcoming incompatibility comes from the life of Nelson Mandela. He was able to forgive his white accusers who falsely imprisoned him for twenty-seven years in South Africa for standing up for the rights of his fellow workers. He forgave the entire White Apartheid Regime, who were in power at that time. When released from prison, he eventually became the president of South Africa, and he named "reconciliation" the primary task of his presidency. He won the Nobel Prize for Peace in 1993. He is quoted as saying: "Forgiveness liberates the soul and removes fear. That's why it's such a powerful weapon!"

The Value of Having Mentors

I have been fortunate to have had wonderful mentors who were willing to walk along with me in my journey in forgiveness. All of them have been humble people of faith who had severe struggles with forgiveness in their own lives. They knew exactly how I was feeling in the middle of my hurts and suffering. They were transparent and vulnerable and openly shared their stories about how they came to forgive the people who harmed them.

A few years ago, I was really struggling with forgiveness in a particular relationship. It was occupying my brain way too much, and I was having trouble "letting it all go."

I was having lunch one day with a good friend who I considered my mentor. I was sharing my struggles to forgive this particular challenging person. My mentor began to ask me some direct questions, and after I answered, he made some observations. He bluntly said, "Greg, you are a Christian person, and you are called to love him." As he was saying this, I was thinking: *What? Love this person who is always trying to control me? Are you kidding me? I cannot stand to even be in his presence!*

The following morning, I was recalling our lunch conversation and praying about what to do next. I was literally at my wit's end. Suddenly, I felt the Lord tapping me on the shoulder. It was as though He was saying, "Listen up!" Over the next few minutes, He lovingly laid out six steps I could take:

1. **"See him through My eyes."** I immediately agreed that Our Lord looks with LOVE on all of us, including this person I was judging at that time. How could I see this person through His eyes? (See 1 John 4:11–12)
2. **"Judge Not!"** I felt God say, "Let Me do all the judging. Judging is not your job, Greg; it's Mine (see Matthew 7:1–2).
3. **"Take the log out of your own eye."** God showed me that I'm not exactly the paragon of virtue either. I too am a sinner. "And why worry about a speck in your friend's eye when you have a log in your own?" (Matthew 7:3)
4. **"Forgive, forgive, forgive!"** The seventy times seven-type of forgiveness is unconditional and is not counted (see Matthew 18:21–22). I interpreted this as "Don't let this guy bug you so much and keep on forgiving."
5. **"Be a prayer commando on his behalf!"** This man has problems, anger, self-image issues, demons all over the place. I felt Jesus calling me to pray and intercede for him. "Ask ME to expel all his demons, and to help him be set free."

6. **"Read Colossians 3:12-15."** These verses pull together all of what we are called to do in forgiving others with tenderhearted mercy.

Because I had been so obsessed with this relationship, initially, I was leery of this new process from Our Lord. I wanted to try it, but I remained a little skeptical. A few days later, I had another encounter with this person. As I observed him and listened to him, I was recounting this process, walking through each step. To my amazement, my former levels of judgment and condemnation began to disappear. I was beginning to see this fellow through the eyes of Christ. I have called this my Eyes of Christ process ever since, and it has worked very well with other people with whom I've had troubles.

Another important aha moment occurred in this story. I eventually began to recognize that seeing this other fellow at his worst reminded me of myself at my worst. The Holy Spirit was working overtime with me in this forgiveness work. I began to forgive both of us.

A wonderful story of forgiveness is portrayed in the book *Unbroken* by Lauren Hillenbrand.[7] A famous Olympic distance runner named Louis Zamperini became an officer in the US Army Air Force in the Pacific, and while on a search-and-rescue mission, he crashed into the ocean. He and other crewmates were lost at sea for forty-seven days, then captured by the Japanese in the Marshall Islands. He was taken to four different prisoner-of-war camps, where he was tortured and beaten by Japanese military personnel, especially by Mutsuhiro Watanabe—due to Zamperini's status as a famous Olympic runner.

After the war, he struggled with PTSD and nightmares regarding his former Japanese captors as he tried to forget his experiences as a POW. He began drinking heavily. In 1949, Louis reluctantly attended a Billy Graham Crusade and became a born-again Christian. He committed his life to Christ, was finally able to forgive his captors, and his nightmares

---

[7] Laura Hillenbrand, *Unbroken: A World War II Story of Survival, Resilience, and Redemption* (Canada: Random House of Canada, 2010).

ceased. He also sent a letter to his former tormentor, telling Watanabe that while he suffered great mistreatment from him, he forgave him.

Spiritual Works of Mercy of the Catholic Church

A few years ago, we were visiting family in Minneapolis, Minnesota. We wanted to attend Mass and found a wonderful French-style Catholic church along the Mississippi River called Our Lady of Lourdes. Sitting in the pew, I quickly noticed two banners just behind altar. On the left was a green banner with *Spiritual Works of Mercy* at the top. On the right was another banner with the words *Corporal Works of Mercy*.

I was riveted to the banner on the left. Since I was thinking and praying a lot about forgiveness issues in my life, I was very interested in the words on the banner. Fortunately, I had pen and paper to write them down; however, I could not actually see all the words until the very end of the Mass. We went back to where we were staying, and I looked them up. Here they are:

1. **Instruct the Ignorant**. In the forgiveness realm, this may mean informing others about the offenses they have perpetrated upon us or others. I have seen folks who are totally oblivious to what they say or do that inflicts hurt and harm on others.
2. **Counsel the Doubtful.** This would normally mean that we could counsel people we know about Our Lord who still have reservations about Him, like Doubting Thomas in the Bible. But if they doubt or argue about how they have hurt us, we also can gently remind them of the impact of their words or actions.
3. **Admonish Sinners**. When we attempt to communicate to our offenders about their hurtful words and behaviors, this is a form of admonishment. Hopefully, we can muster as much kindness as we can in delivering the message. In my own life, I have seen how some fully accept this admonishment and apologize, while others reject, ignore, or become defensive when they receive even one iota of critical input about their behavior. At times,

our tough love for others may compel us to try to assist others who are out of line in what they say and do.

4. **Bear Wrongs Patiently.** The message here is to not overreact or blow our tops at the slightest provocation. In business, I adopted a twenty-four-hour rule, which meant I would not respond to situations that angered me for at least twenty-four hours. I'd often prepare an email that was going to skewer someone else about something I thought they did, then look at it again twenty-four hours later. I was able to calm down in the interim and realize the correspondence sent in anger would have created all kinds of problems. Almost none of these emails ever got sent!

5. **Forgive Offenses Willingly.** We are all human, and we all make mistakes. If we remain on our high horse of self-righteous indignation, we are not in a mindset of forgiving easily. Ronald Rolheiser, in his book *Sacred Fire,* encourages us to become "automatic forgivers." We can train ourselves to forgive quickly and easily. In so doing, we take on the very mind and heart of Jesus.

6. **Comfort the Afflicted.** In way too many cases, I jumped to conclusions about another person without understanding anything about why they might have done what they did to harm me. In a few cases, I've learned details and realized that they had endured unimaginable harm themselves. They are afflicted, and I can attempt to comfort them by showing mercy, compassion, and empathy. I can become a better listener without jumping to judgments and condemnation. I can walk with them as a wing person when no one else is willing to do so.

7. **Pray for the Living and the Dead.** As Christians, we are called to a life of prayer. We can certainly pray for the deceased, who may not have ever formed a relationship with Jesus. We can attempt to pray them into heaven! We can pray for the people around us right now, especially the people we struggle to forgive. We can pray and intercede for them right now.

Small Group Support and Encouragement

Many Christians are part of a small group or a Bible study that meets regularly. Participants share their lives with others, and close friendships are developed. As people get to know one another, they feel comfortable sharing their deepest problems. Issues are discussed openly. Honesty, confidentiality, and vulnerability are keys to the ongoing success of these groups.

For some of the members in the group, unforgiveness can be a big problem. The group can listen intently to difficulties. Others in the group can share what they have done to forgive others or themselves. The ability to share about forgiveness issues becomes a huge relief to the person struggling. It is said that "a burden shared is halved."

If a member of the group is open to suggestions, they can listen and try to employ the ideas they have learned from the group. All the conversations should begin and end with prayer. All the conversations are confidential. There hopefully is regular use of the Holy Scriptures to discern the call to forgiveness. In these forums, mutual encouragement runs high, since we all know how tough it is to forgive. And there may even be some "tough love" if a member continues to reject or refuse any efforts to forgive. Their feet can be held to the fire, fully knowing that all the members only want the best for one another. We all seek healing and freedom from the ravages of unforgiveness.

Members can pray with and over one another to invoke the power and grace of the Holy Spirit. In our challenges with forgiveness, we need God's help! As Proverbs 27:17 says, "As iron sharpens iron, so a friend sharpens a friend."

Forgiving Ourselves Too

We lived in Orange County, California, for close to forty years, before moving about six years ago. I was a financial advisor during most of those years. For the last fifteen years, I was affiliated with a small, independent financial planning firm. It was by far the best place I'd ever worked. It seemed God-ordained to me for many good reasons.

While at this firm, I had a large corner office, changed cars too often, and lived at the top of a hill, with a killer view of the local mountains. I joined several private country clubs in succession. In those days, golf was extremely important to me, and I spent a lot of time "enjoying" this hobby. In reality, it was more of an obsession.

It became important for me to "keep up with the Joneses." In a place like Orange County, it was quite easy to get caught up in the lifestyle. I was crazy busy all the time, with activities starting at 7:00 a.m. almost every day of the week. I began to think of myself as "OC Greg." I bought into a worldly lifestyle hook, line, and sinker.

If I had to do it all over again, I would have avoided a lot of the activities which were so important to me back then. I have had many regrets about how I conducted myself.

You may have had similar experiences. You might be asking yourself:

- What was I thinking when I did that?
- How dumb was I anyway?
- I can't believe I allowed myself to get so caught up in the world.
- Not exactly my proudest moment, right?

I have named these episodes as being stuck in the GSRR's: guilt, shame, regrets, and remorse. We wish we could do it over again, but the past is gone. We cannot do anything about the past, so it's best to move on with life today. As they say, it's all "water under the bridge."

We all make mistakes. We are human, forgiving ourselves is a big deal, and it's hard to do. In my view, too many of us are still stuck way back in the past. We just cannot seem to erase our mistakes.

A good friend of mine is really good at beating himself up over the mistakes of his past life. He has trouble letting go of the way he used to be. I've encouraged him to "move on" from the past and live in the joy and peace that Jesus provides here and now. This is really good advice for me as well.

Alexander Pope once said, "To err is human; to forgive is divine." This includes forgiving ourselves. And do we realize how much our Lord has already forgiven us?

In the story of the paralyzed man in Mark 2:5, Jesus said to the man: "My child, your sins are forgiven." Likewise, those of us who demonstrate great faith and repentance can prepare ourselves to fully accept Jesus' forgiveness. Many people I know are still stuck in the GSRR's because they have not forgiven themselves or accepted the forgiveness that Jesus has freely offered. Let us all commit to getting "unstuck" from our past mistakes and bask in the love and joy of Jesus right now.

Decision Day

In chapter 7, we looked at the realizations we come to in order to forgive. One big one is that we are destroying ourselves from within, while harboring all the nasty ravages of unforgiveness. It affects our minds, our bodies, and our souls.

We all come to a day of reckoning when we will ask ourselves: Will I forgive this person for what they did to me? Will I forgive myself for what I did? This day is decision day. I came to a few important insights on these decisions for myself:

- I became really tired of judging others.
- I did not like being angry so often. A friend called me an "anger expert."
- I got tired of replaying events of the past, which were all gone.
- I realized that I was missing the joy and peace of living in the Lord here and now.

- I realized that Our Lord will make amends, will judge us all, will hold us all accountable—all in His timing. I no longer needed to plot revenge.
- I came to the place where I said: "Enough is enough. Life is too short to be harboring any ill will toward anyone else or myself. Spending any more time or energy on unforgiveness is a colossal waste of time. I can be serving God and His people instead."
- I really wanted to set free from the "prison" of unforgiveness. As the expression goes: "We drink the poison and hope the other person dies." So, who is suffering here? We are, not the offender.
- I prayed for my well-being to be restored. I've learned that forgiveness does provide that wonderful restoration. It's like being released from prison after years of being locked up in solitary confinement.

I was encouraged by the following Scriptures:

> Today I have given you the choice between life and death, between blessings and curses. Now I call on heaven and earth to witness to the choice you made. Oh, that you would choose life, so that you and your descendants might live! You can make this choice by loving the LORD your God, obeying him, and committing yourself firmly to him. This is the key to your life. (Deuteronomy 30:19–20)

> Since we believe that Christ died for all, we also believe we have died to our old life. He died for everyone so that those who receive his new life no longer live for themselves. Instead, they will live for Christ, who died and was raised for them. This means that anyone who belongs to Christ has become a new person. The old life is gone; a new life has begun. (2 Corinthians 5:14–15, 17)

I love the story of the bleeding woman in Mark 5:21–34. A woman had suffered for twelve years with constant bleeding. She saw doctors and spent all her money on finding a cure, but she was no better. In fact, she had gotten worse. I think there is a remarkable parallel here to our struggles with unforgiveness, which might have been going on for many decades. I'm constantly amazed at the stories I hear from people who have not spoken to family members (or others) for years over a minor disagreement. I hear people say: "I'm never speaking to this person ever again!"

The bleeding woman hears about Jesus, comes up behind him in a crowded room, and touches his robe. She says to herself: "If I can just touch his robe, I will be healed." Immediately, her bleeding stopped, and she felt in her body that she had been healed of her terrible condition. Likewise, Jesus will heal us of our unforgiveness.

Jesus quickly realized his healing power had gone out of him, so he turned around in the crowd and asked: "Who touched my robe?" Jesus kept looking around for the person who had touched his robe. The frightened woman was trembling at the realization of what had happened to her, and she fell to her knees in front of him and told him what she had done. Then Jesus said to her: "Daughter, your faith has made you well. Go in peace. Your suffering is over."

Reminders on Forgiveness for the Road Ahead:

1. Lean on Jesus to help us with forgiveness.
2. Study the Scriptures on forgiveness. Put these into practice.
3. Do not judge, condemn, or badmouth your offenders.
4. Stop replaying your grievance story in your minds—or out loud.
5. Apologize for your own sins and wrongdoing.
6. Be humble and check your ego. Get rid of righteous indignation.
7. Say NO to revenge!
8. Cut others some slack. Look for the best in others.
9. Reconcile if possible. Be the first one to reach out. Bury the hatchet.

10. Pray and intercede for your offenders. They need your prayers.
11. Bear wrongs patiently.
12. Incompatibility is OK. It's not a crime to not like some folks.
13. Become less thin-skinned to the words and behaviors of others.
14. Forgive seventy times seven.
15. Know how much you've been forgiven yourself.
16. Love your enemies.
17. Remember that you are a new creation in Christ.
18. Replace callousness and hard-heartedness with tenderhearted mercy and compassion.

Take Courage!

In John 16:33, Jesus tells us, "Here on earth, you will have many trials and sorrows. But take heart [be of good cheer], because I have overcome the world." Here Jesus here is inviting us to take courage, knowing that we won't be alone in our struggles to forgive if we ask Him to help us.

I hope this book serves as a guide for you on how to go about working on forgiveness. The ideas suggested have helped me on my own journey. Others have commented on the benefits as well. I pray that you become successful in forgiveness. Please let me know how you are doing. Glory to Jesus!

For Reflection

1. Have you invited Jesus to help you with your struggles in forgiveness? Do you realize that He has His hands outstretched to you right now?
2. Are you brave enough to touch the hem of Jesus's robe today, in order to forgive everyone who has ever hurt you? If not, what is holding you back?
3. Make a decision today to forgive—it's the best gift you could ever give yourself!

Thank You, Lord, for the lives we have in You. We thank You for Your amazing love. We thank You for all ways You have forgiven us throughout our entire lives. Help us to forgive as You forgive.

We ask You now for Your supernatural grace and power to overcome the hurts and harm others have put upon us. In You alone, we can overcome the barriers and strongholds seated deep within us. Deliver us, Lord, from all the bondage of unforgiveness. Lord, You even forgave the people who were crucifying You on the Cross!

Lord, we ask that You anoint us with Your Holy Spirit to love when we are tempted to hate, to turn the other cheek when we are tempted to retaliate, to forgive others when it makes no possible sense to do so. In You, O Lord, we live and move and have our being. Thank You, Lord for the power and grace You continuously pour out upon us.

We pray this day for Your abundant strength and courage. Give us a true desire to forgive. We know You desire to help us to be set free. Empower us, Lord, to do our part. Amen.

MORE RESOURCES ON FORGIVENESS

In my own study on forgiveness, I've come across other resources which I've found helpful. All of us approach forgiveness in our own way. I hope you may find these helpful as well.

Books

- *Forgive for Good* by Dr. Fred Luskin
- *Forgiveness Is a Choice* by Robert D. Enright, PhD
- *Let It Go Workbook* by Pastor T.D. Jakes
- *Sacred Fire* by Ronald Rolheiser
- *Freedom Is a Choice* by Robert Enright

Videos, Podcasts, and Websites

- *How to Forgive* from the Good Catholic (A fourteen-day program on forgiveness)
- *21 Days to Freedom in Forgiveness* by Greg Aitkens (found on the EntertheHealingRoom.com, under the MORE tab)
- Prager University on YouTube featuring Dr. Steven Marmer, UCLA Medical School, on Exoneration, Forbearance, and Release
- Love Your Enemies on HeGetsus.com

ABOUT THE AUTHOR

Greg Aitkens graduated with his bachelor's and master's degrees in Recreation and was in charge of running large municipal recreation programs. He then began a career as a Certified Financial Planner in Orange County, California. He is the founder of the Orange County chapter of Christians in Commerce, now called Worklight (www.Worklight.org). He has written more than eighty reflections on the topic of forgiveness and conducted many workshops on this topic. He offers one-on-one coaching for people who struggle with unforgiveness and long to be set free. Greg and his wife, Ginny, have been married for more than fifty years and have three adult children and two grandchildren (with a third on the way). You can learn more about Greg by visiting his website, www.EnterTheHealingRoom.com.

www.ingramcontent.com/pod-product-compliance
Lightning Source LLC
LaVergne TN
LVHW011736060526
838200LV00051B/3197